Pocket Size Interview Guide

Crystal Vaughan

Copyright © 2016 Crystal Vaughan

All rights reserved.

ISBN-10: 1537015338
ISBN-13: 978-1537015330

DEDICATION

This book is dedicated to everyone who participated in my interview skills workshop. It was your questions and brilliant minds that inspired me to write this book.

CONTENTS

	Acknowledgments	i
	Introduction	1
1	Interviewing as an Art	5
2	Information is Power!	7
3	Be Prepared	19
4	STAR Method of Interviewing	33
5	Twenty-Five Interview Questions and What the Interviewer is Looking for in Your Answer	39
6	Illegal Interview Questions	61
7	Choosing the Right Questions to Ask	65
8	Closing the Interview	71
9	The Follow Up	75
10	A Brief Social Media Discussion	79
11	Interview Types	83
12	Fast Tips for a Second Interview	91
13	A Quick Overview	97
	25 Questions Worksheet	99
	Helpful Resources	113

ACKNOWLEDGMENTS

I would like to acknowledge every Human Resource person who has ever helped me during my career. They imparted a lot of information with me regarding the interview process.

INTRODUCTION

If you are reading this I'm sure you've stopped by my blog at least once, http://withCrystal.com. If you haven't, you should visit; there is some handy information on job hunting there. I also direct you to some of my favorite sites that have a lot of information regarding interviewing, job hunting, and sites that have free educational courses.

For those who don't know me from Joe or Jill. I am Crystal, I run the blog mentioned above and work a day job that I really love; however, that job will be going away in 2018. And that, my dear, is how I came to write this book.

It began with the invitation to lead the workshop on Interviewing Skills at the facility that I work at. The supervisors are very gracious people who through no fault of their own, are in the same boat that the employees are, facing our inevitable shut down. So, to help the staff that work under them, my employers are giving us every opportunity to better ourselves through knowledge, so that we are more capable of finding jobs when closure hits us in 2018.

I, of course, accepted the invitation, despite my reservations about standing in front of people and speaking. Strike the word reservations, despite my paralyzing fear of standing in front of people and speaking. Helping and teaching others is something that I'm passionate about, if that means that I have to overcome a few fears in order to do so, then so be it.

In the time that I taught this workshop, the discussions I had with the attendees were brilliant, and I found myself doing more and more research in an effort to be able to answer everyone's questions. I found a passion for learning as much as I can about interviewing. There has to be a formula to it, some way to make yourself so good at it, that you are practically guaranteed the job!

So through my research and life experience I found that, unfortunately, there's really not a formula.

I know, I know, trust me I was disappointed too. But there is just too much human error in the interviewing process, BUT there are ways to prepare yourself into being the best candidate possible. That preparation will give you an edge over nearly everyone else who shows up at the interview (unless of course they too have read this book, in which case may the best applicant win!)

So, that is enough about me and how I got to this place, in front of my computer typing away in order to give you the knowledge that I now possess. I hope it helps you as much as I hope it has helped my (former) coworkers who participated in my Interview Skills workshop.

1 INTERVIEWING AS AN ART

Being artistic is a serious skill. But every artist at one point or another was drawing stick figures with their crayons. They had a passion about art that caused them to dig deep and decide to work at it; to try different mediums and to practice. Ask any artist you know if they had any disastrous creations. If they are being honest, then their answer will be a resounding YES!

Know this, you will make mistakes. A great artist has learned how to incorporate their mistakes into the masterpiece and I hope that the skills and lessons that are presented to you in this book will give you the tools you need in order to do the same. It is one thing to let a blunder in your answer stop you in your tracks, but when you learn to incorporate your mistakes into your masterpiece you will be able to smooth over that blunder or at least de-emphasize it.

There is a mantra that you will notice throughout the text of these pages and that is:

PRACTICE PRACTICE PRACTICE!!!

It is integral that you practice your interview skills. You can have all the knowledge in the world regarding interviewing, but unless you practice it will not do you a bit of good. Like an artist, someone can read thousands of books on various art forms, creations, and techniques, but unless they are crafting along the way to learn these forms and techniques, then they will never truly be artists.

You aren't looking to be an artist. You are looking to be employed, but the thought process is the same with the purpose of practicing.

And while my goal isn't to make you an artist per se, my goal is to help you get many many steps closer to being employed.

The main focus of this book is to help you during the actual interview. I do however, offer bits of advice on other areas leading up to and coming away from the interview. That is because while the interview itself is a onetime (but very important) event during your job search, there are many factors that can affect how the interview goes and how it is viewed in hindsight by the interviewers.

2 INFORMATION IS POWER!

In an interview setting this statement is incredibly true and incredibly powerful.

There are people who apply to jobs and get called for an interview and never even think to do their homework. They don't do anything more than barely skim over the job description.

Research the company?

Who has time for that?

If you want that job you are interviewing for, then YOU HAVE TIME FOR THAT. If you are one of those people who never thought to research the place that they are applying to, shame on you, but make me a promise and do better before your next big interview.

But first, why is information about a company good to

have before going in for the interview?

If you are truly passionate about wanting to work with this company you will want to cater your answers to their interview questions to fit the culture and values of the company. This will give you an edge over equally qualified competitors who do not do their research. They may have fit in just as well as you will, but they won't be able to *show* the interviewer that in their answers. With the knowledge that you will gain through your research you will be able to make your answers feel like they are coming from someone who belongs with the company.

When you receive the phone call to schedule your interview, you will need to:

Get started gathering information by:

Researching the company:

- Find their website
- Facebook page/Social Sites
- Mission & Vision Statements
- In the news
- Ask current employees about the work culture there (don't feel comfortable approaching current employees? I have a few extra tips on this later)
- Read the job description you are applying to until you practically have it memorized

- - o Compare this job description to other companies advertising for the same position; this can help point out differences in their expectations.
- Study all their currently advertised jobs posted and/or general company advertisements
- Review all the information that you have gathered and ask yourself this question: What seems to be important to this company?
- Pay attention to buzz words and repeated information.

Website

Most companies have websites now. A quick web search should turn up their website fairly easily. Pay close attention to the site. Is it up-to-date? Can you tell that it is being cared for?

Either way you will want to read the information on the website, but do be cautious, if it seems to be seriously out of date with broken links and outdated information, you may want to take the information that you gather here with a grain of salt and know that the values, ideals, and culture of this company could have changed in the time that it has taken their website to run down.

If the site is up-to-date, looks great, and you can tell someone is constantly caring for it, then rest assured that this information will be very valuable. But again, know that this is the face that the company wants the rest of the world to see, and sometimes what is inside of a company is a little bit different than what they project outwardly. This is why learning about the company's culture is so important.

The best places to look at on their website to learn the best information about a company is on their about us page, vision/mission statements, customer reviews, department pages (these usually have a little information about each department), etc. Try your best to go over the majority of the website, but I do realize that some sites are massive and if it is a company that has several locations across the country some of the information you find on their website might not be relevant to the location that you are applying to.

Now, not all websites will have all the information listed that you want to look for, and that is okay. You may be able to find that information out through other means.

Bonus Tip: See if the company keeps an updated blog on their website, blogs are easy to update and if they are blogging frequently this may be a good place to get information. Also, some of the employees may keep their own blogs, keep an eye out for posts by current or previous employees that may give you some insight on the company's culture.

Facebook/Social Sites

Now that you've looked over the company's website, see if they have a Facebook page.

Side note: there are some companies that may not have a website and only have a Facebook page and vice versa.

Their Facebook page will be a plethora of information if they have a lot of interaction with customers/clients on there. You can get a read on how their fan base feels about them and see how they respond. There may be more up-to-date information on their Facebook page since Facebook is so easy to update and keep active. I also suggest following their page so that you can keep up with any news that they put out. This will help keep you aware of anything newsworthy that comes up between now and interview day. But, do realize that by liking their page you are making your own social media profile much easier to find for them to review (but more on that later). You can repeat this process with other social sites such as LinkedIn, Twitter, Instagram, YouTube, etc.

Mission and Vision Statements

Make sure on each outlet you find the company you are researching you look to see if their mission and vision statements are the same. Some companies regularly update their statements and you may be able to see how the statements have changed over the years if you can find a place where they haven't updated them yet. This can give you some understanding on how the company is growing and changing. Are they headed in a direction that you are interested in going? If so, what can you bring to the table to help them on their way?

Culture

I debated discussing this topic first, but the website and social media pages will help to give you a little bit of a window into the company's culture which resulted in this being the fourth topic in this Chapter instead of the first.

Knowing the culture of a company is critical during your job search. If their culture does not fit you PLEASE do not work there. Always remember that even if you get a job offer, if it isn't a good fit for you, then you do **not** have to say yes. I cannot reiterate this enough, it is horrible to get stuck in a job where you are miserable and don't fit in with the people who work there. You become desperate to get another job and the cycle can continue.

I will acknowledge there are some situations where you may wind up taking a job that you aren't quite a perfect fit for in order to have a paycheck coming in. And that is okay and understandable.

If you find yourself in the situation mentioned above, I want you to keep in mind that you do not want to repeat the scenario in the future. To avoid this keep a list of companies that you would be interested in working at. Periodically check up on them so you can apply to positions that you have the qualifications for. If you are unhappy with your job, but not in the middle of a heavy job hunt I recommend doing this so that you won't miss out on an opportunity to work where you will be happy. It also helps you to know what is available should your current employment end unexpectedly, as that is type of situation that can land you in a position where you are unhappy and desperate for a paycheck.

I do NOT want you to end up with a job where you are dissatisfied, especially if you are using my information to do well in the interview to obtain this job. You will spend a minimum of 40 hours at work (unless you work part-time) each week. That is a huge chunk of your life. It is not worth it to be somewhere that you are miserable for that large amount of time. Sometimes you will need to cut your losses if you find yourself in that type of position and begin the job hunt again. Now, I'm not saying to quit your job while hunting for another. Unless you are VERY financially secure, it is best to conduct your job hunt while in your current position.

Finding out the culture of a place can be tricky; you really have to get on the inside to get this question answered, which is great if you are fairly close with someone who works at the company. However, it can be done if you don't.

Use your earlier research from the website and social media sites to see how the company represents itself. Check out websites like Glassdoor.com and Indeed.com to see what current and former employees say about the company.

Go on LinkedIn and professionally reach out to employees of the company. Don't be demanding or creepy about it though. Just a nice intro as to why you are contacting them and a thank you for their time. If you get a reply, great! If you do not, don't keep contacting them. If you do get a job at the company you don't want your coworkers to think of you as that weirdo who wouldn't back off from sending them incessant messages.

Some other places to look for indicators of a company's culture are press releases and news articles about the company. Don't let these little gems of information pass you by!

Other Jobs Posted/Company Ads

Read other job ads that they currently have posted, this will give you some insight into company lingo/buzzwords that they are fond of. It can also give you a sign on whether the company is in the middle of an overhaul. An indicator of a company going through major internal changes is if there are tons upon tons of jobs being advertised from a company that generally only has a few positions open at a time. In this case you may be walking into an environment of change. Which is great for those who love change and innovation, this would be a place where one could leave their own stamp on the job. However, it could be an indicator of something amiss. Just use your best judgment and you should be able to get a feel for things during the interview when you utilize the opportunity to ask them questions at the interview's end.

Company ads will also give you an idea of the company's preferred lingo/buzzwords. It also may clue you in on a new direction or project that the position you are applying for may be involved in. If you think it is the latter, do a lot of research on that front and be prepared to bring it up during the interview. This will make you look knowledgeable and interested in the position.

Job Description

You will definitely want to read the job description to the job that you are applying for. Make sure that you highlight any areas that you may have questions about. If these questions are not answered during the interview process you will want to bring them up with the interviewer before you leave.

Compare the job description to other companies' descriptions that are advertising for the same or similar positions. This will give you an idea of how this company differs from others and what their expectations will be from you in this position. Is it greater than other companies or less? If it is greater, are you looking for a position with more responsibility (and will the company be willing to appropriately compensate you for doing more work than you would elsewhere)? If so then this may be the place to apply to. If not, look to those other companies advertising the same position, but with fewer expectations/more appropriate compensation.

What seems important?
After going through all of your research, pay attention to and highlight what seems important to the company. It will be the things that come up again and again. Do they have their vision and mission front and center on all of their online profiles? Chances are they take them very seriously and you should focus on information that you find about the company that lines up with those values and study them prior to your interview.

Buzzwords
Words that the company uses in their lingo over and over again are good words to pick up and use during your interview, especially those that apply to the position that you are trying to obtain. Just don't overuse them and make sure you know what they mean!

Now that you know how to gain information on the company keep in mind that the information you have is only powerful if you use it. When you are practicing the interview questions in Chapter 5 be sure to use the knowledge you have gained about the company in your answers. By practicing in this way the information will flow more easily in your answers and not seem as forced or rehearsed. Think about the easy flow of casual conversation versus the stilted speech of a nervous student who has quickly memorized a speech to recite. You want the easy flow of casual conversation throughout the interview. Just not too casual, it is an interview after all.

3 BE PREPARED

You always want to be prepared before walking into an interview setting. Chapter 2 covered the research preparation work you will want to do prior to going into an interview, but what other things do you need to do before you are ready for that big day?

Bring your application and resume.

First you will want to bring an updated application and a tailored resume with you if they request it. Personally, I recommend bringing both with you even if they do not request it, just in case you need them.

Why do you want to bring both?

There are differences between your application and resume that are subtle, but important. That is why it is important to bring a copy of each.

The application is a form that the company gives you and requests you to fill out. It is homogenous, leaves little room for explanation, is mostly full of legal information, is easily comparable between applicants, and is sometimes filled out on-site. Because of that last one, I recommend filling out a state job application (these are some of the most detailed applications that you can find) and bring it with you. This way, if you become nervous during any interview questions, you have all of your work history information at your fingertips and aren't um-ing and ah-ing your way through a question.

The resume is a document unique to you and unique to this position. (I recommend that you have one resume per every position that you apply to). Resumes change depending on the job and company that you are applying to and they can provide more detail in the areas that you want to highlight. Resumes can be presented in a more professional manner than an application and are sent by you to the potential employer versus being requested, although some companies will require a resume be sent in with your application and cover letter.

Before sending either anywhere you need to make sure you have had both your resume and your application proofread by someone you trust and that you have made any appropriate changes.

Know all your employment facts.

This is why I stress bringing an up-to-date complete state application with you. Coming prepared shows initiative to your potential employers and it helps should you become nervous about being "put on the spot" during the interview process.

Know what you will want to emphasize about each position that you held previously that relates to the job you are currently applying for. Practice working these emphasis points in on various practice interview questions. I go over 25 of the most popular interview questions in Chapter 5.

Be sure that your employment facts are accurate. Many potential employers will go back and do their own research to ensure that you were answering questions factually. Stretching the truth or telling an outright lie <u>will</u> cost you the position.

And it won't just hurt you now, it could also potentially cost you down the road if the truth surfaces after you've been with the company for a while. It's not worth lying to obtain the job, as that will mar any chances you have with other positions at this company in the future. You also ruin your chances with those particular interviewers. They could move to other companies that you would have been interested in and they will most likely remember you if you blew it in this spectacular kind of a way.

Know the location of the interview.

This one should be a no brainer, but you would be surprised at how many interviewees I've seen arrive late because they couldn't be bothered to scope out the route to the company ahead of time. Granted, some circumstances can arise that will cause you to be late, if that is the case give a courteous call to the Human Resources Department and let them know. However, most situations that will cause you to be late can be avoided.

Answer these questions about the location prior to your interview date:

1. Where is the interview taking place and at what time exactly?

2. How long does it typically take to get there?

3. Will traffic be a problem during this time of day?

I recommend that you allow yourself time to find a restroom to freshen up prior to your interview; this is especially important during the heat of summer and during bad weather days. I would also allow at least 10 minutes before the interview to have extra time to review any information that is given to you prior to getting in the hot seat. At many companies I've interviewed at they will give you a more in depth job description to review before the interview or they may have a work sample for you to complete. Some companies will tell you upfront that you need to come in early for various reasons, just be sure to allow yourself enough time to be on time to a little bit early.

Don't arrive too early though. It can be awkward if you are sitting in a lobby area for 30 minutes or longer while waiting for your interview due to you being early. It is a different situation entirely if it is the company that is running behind causing your extended wait.

Side Note: I hope I don't have to say this to you, but I'm going to put it out there anyway, if the company is running behind, do not be impatient or rude. If you are going to need to leave to be somewhere then be polite and kindly ask if you can reschedule due to the delay. However, do try not to schedule anything else on the day of your interview, any appointments before can cause you to be late, and appointments scheduled for after can cause you undue stress as you worry about rushing through the interview so you aren't late to your next appointment.

A few interesting employment facts to help you on your path to being prepared for your interview and job search were found on a 2014 survey from JobVite.com, TheUndercoverRecruiter.com and Work4labs.com:

- A recruiter spends roughly 5 to 7 seconds looking at your resume. So make sure your resume says wow, is easy to read, and that your most important points pop on the page.

- Unprofessional email addresses cause 76% of resumes to be discarded. There are too many free options for email addresses to have this happen to you. So go create a professional email address and use it for your job search.

Side Note: While I do recommend having a professional email address for you to use on your applications and resume, I do not advise using your current work email address. You never know when you could lose access to it from an unexpected layoff, etc. Then you could potentially miss out on a job opportunity and never know that you did.

- Just 35% of job applicants are qualified for the jobs they apply to. So be sure you research those qualifications, if you are truly qualified, you just came out ahead of 65% of your competition!

Side Note: If you meet the majority of the qualifications but there is a bullet or two in the job description that you've never done before, you shouldn't let that hold you back from trying for the job. If you are a year short on the experience necessary I would also give it a shot. You know how to do the majority of the work, so during the interview emphasize those points and talk about how you would quickly and readily take on the other tasks that you have little to no experience with. If you act excited about the prospect, they will be less concerned with those few things you can't do and focus more on how well you will fit with the company.

- I'm sure this number has drastically increased in the last few years, but in 2014 68% of employers will find you on Facebook and 93% of recruiters will look at your social media profile. So spend some time researching how best to present yourself online and then follow through with the advice you find. I give a brief amount of advice in Chapter 10, however, social media job hunting tips can vary by industry.

Prepare your body and mind

To further expand upon preparing your mind in Chapter 5 I will share 25 of the most common interview questions along with explanations of why the recruiters ask these particular questions and what they are looking for in your answers.

Your Attire and Appearance

You need to dress appropriately for the industry, for an interview this will be a step up from what you would be wearing day to day in your job. Don't wear a suit to an interview at a company that is very low key and relaxed with a very comfortable daily dress, but also don't wear short shorts and a tank top to that same interview. This is another spot where your research about the company's culture will come into play.

Your personal grooming and cleanliness needs to be impeccable. Don't walk into the interview after working in the garden all day. Smelling of body odor and having visible dirt on you and under your nails is a huge turn off not only to the recruiter, but to potential coworkers that you will run into along the way. While you need to be clean and well groomed, I advise against using soaps and perfumes/colognes with strong smells. Actually, I advise against perfume and cologne period, you don't want to run into an interviewer who has an allergy or is sensitive to smells. They will be more focused on not feeling well than on what you are bringing to the table. The last thing you want to do is to distract them from your great qualifications and rapport with them.

Body Language

Be sure that your body language is relaxed, demonstrates confidence, and doesn't make you appear to be unapproachable. In other words, I want you to look exactly the opposite from how you will probably feel.

- Use good posture, sit straight, look attentive

- Keep eye contact, especially during the handshake (if you shake their hand, more on that later).

- Don't stare. Too much eye contact can start to become uncomfortable, really it can, try it with a friend if you don't believe me.

- Don't use aggressive motions, this can cause unintended feelings of hostility.

- Keep your arms and chest open and your back straight. Doing this makes you seem approachable as closed arms signify that you are not open for conversation.

- ONLY nod at the MOST effective points.
    - Please do not nod at everything that the interviewer says, this will give you the appearance of a bobble head doll, which I'm assuming you are not, and will distract the interviewer from your answers.

- Do NOT fidget. This will also be a distraction for the interviewers.
    - Do not put your hands under the table to try to hide your fidgeting. This looks so weird from the other side of the table. Try it with a friend just to see how weird it looks. I'll wait…good, now you know

why you should not do that.

- While you are not fidgeting, try not to be overly stiff. This goes hand in hand with the closed arms in causing you to seem unapproachable.

- Match your tone and expression to your answer. When you are talking about your passions be passionate, don't drone on in a flat tone of voice. This is contradictory to your feelings and creates an odd interview atmosphere.

The main focus on your personal body language is to make sure that what you are displaying will make the interviewer feel comfortable with you. You do not want to be doing things that will distract them from your answers and the good rapport that you are trying to develop with him/her. This rapport is crucial in showing the interviewer how well you would fit in at the company.

During your interview you will begin with greetings and introductions, this is the place where many interviewers will go to shake your hand. Be sure you have a good strong handshake. Don't be limp like a dead fish out of water, but also don't grip so hard that they feel bruised afterwards.

If you go to shake their hand and you can sense that they aren't someone who likes to shake hands (this could be due to coming from a different culture or being opposed to germs, it isn't necessarily an affront to you as a person) don't push the issue or you risk going straight into creating a hostile atmosphere in the interview room. I want you to start off on the right foot. Any blunders early on in the interview setting can cause you to feel overly nervous and effect the entire outcome and your performance during the interview. First impressions and all…

When introducing yourself be warm, friendly, and personable. Act like you like the interviewer, this can be hard to do when nerves are fluttering like crazy, but it helps to break the tension that you are feeling. Don't act like they are your best friend, being too chummy too soon can come off as a bit odd to some people.

Now, while you will want to be focused on your body language and what it is telling the interviewer, you also need to tune into their body language so you know what they are trying to tell you.

If they begin to look tired or bored, you may be answering one of their questions in a boring or typical way. This could be an indicator that they've heard this answer a dozen times today and it is becoming overdone. Quickly rethink how you are answering and see if this is an appropriate place to pull from another work/life experience. Be sure to give a good story of how you achieved what they are asking for; use the STAR Method from Chapter 4. This shows a true example of what you are capable of doing versus just reciting a list of skills and accomplishments.

A bored expression may also be an indicator that you are going around a question without truly answering it. If you find yourself faced with a question that you genuinely do not know the answer to or do not have the experience to answer, just be honest. Don't waste your time or the interviewer's time. The time during your interview is valuable and it is time that you can use to emphasize the skills and qualifications that you do have on other questions.

If they are looking puzzled, there might be a possibility of you misunderstanding the question. I have seen interview questions that were worded in an odd way. This wording makes it hard for the interviewee (that would be you) to understand just what the recruiter is looking for. If this is the case, don't hesitate to ask for clarification, it is better to get the clarification and answer the question the way they need it answered than to leave them with something that doesn't demonstrate why they should choose you for the job.

If the interviewer looks shocked or appalled at your answer, you may need to rethink what you just said and clarify for the interviewer. It may be that nerves have caused you to slip up and say something that perhaps you shouldn't have. If this is the case, apologize, take a deep breath and try again.

Throughout the entire interview process make sure to be polite and use proper grammar this includes initial contacts from the company to set up the interview, the interview itself, and any follow-up communications. Give your courteousness to all staff members, from the receptionist to the hiring manager. Many companies will look to see how you treat all the staff and/or clients that you come into contact with throughout the entire process. If you are rude to the receptionist, then you have just put a black mark against yourself in the possibility of gaining employment with that company.

When you are exiting the interview, no matter how you feel the interview went, gather your belongings calmly, stand up smoothly, smile, say your farewells, and if appropriate shake everyone's hand and thank them. Even if you feel you did poorly, leave the interview in a confident manner. The interviewer may have thought that you did well, but a negative exit could leave a lasting impact resulting in the interviewer doubting how they felt about your performance.

4 STAR METHOD OF INTERVIEWING

So before we get into the most commonly asked interview questions in Chapter 5, I'd first like to talk to you about the STAR method of interviewing. I first learned of this method when I took an interview skills course at the last company I worked for. The Human Resources manager was a huge fan of this method and it is easy to see why. The STAR method allows you to really drive home the point that you have not only the experience the company needs, but the problem solving skills that are beneficial in nearly every situation you could find yourself in.

By practicing using the STAR method when answering behavioral interview questions you should be prepared for your interview when the big day arrives.

What does STAR mean anyway?
S – Situation
T – Task
A – Action
R – Result

Situation: You will want to make sure that you go into enough detail about the situation that you were faced with for the interviewer to be able to visualize what is happening. Stay away from generic answers, the purpose of STAR is personalization.

Task (also can be known as **T**he problem): What was the outcome you were working towards? Or, what was the problem you were trying to solve?

Action: What action did you take? List specific steps and be sure to point out what your particular contribution was to solving the problem or completing the task.

Result: What was the result of your action? Make sure you take credit for what you did in obtaining the result. Use I, and not we, even when describing your work in a group project. You want to put the emphasis on the work that you did, but do acknowledge that you were a team member on the project. You don't want the interviewer to see you as someone who tries to steal credit either. Try to include more than one positive outcome from your action in the situation.

Sample Behavioral Based Question and S.T.A.R. Answer Technique:

Question: Tell me about a time you demonstrated leadership skills.

Answer:

S   In my last position I was a member of the Creative Dream Team. I had many goals as a team member, one of which was improving employee morale across campus.

T   In order to do this each of us brought ideas to the table regarding morale issues that we had personally witnessed. The issue that I was focused on was communication between departments and between supervisors and their staff.

A   To learn more about what communication issues there seemed to be I led a team discussion on what issues they had seen and developed a survey to go out to all staff on campus.

R   The survey results quickly confirmed my suspicions of staff in every department feeling left out of vital communications. With this information I was able to help lead the team in developing a scorecard indicator for the facility to work on in order to improve communication across campus. The results of working on communication were improved morale and better communication between staff and their supervisors.

Now, you may read the above sample question and wonder how in the world you can cover all of those areas when put on the spot in an interview situation.

Guess what? You aren't going to be able to and that's okay, because most people wouldn't be able to when put on the spot. That is why you will need to...PRACTICE!

You may not know exactly which behavioral questions you are going to be asked. Chapter 5 does have some of the most common questions, but each interviewer is unique so every interview will be as well.

If, after reading Chapter 5, you still want to practice more industry specific questions (which is a great idea!) then just do a quick internet search for "most common interview questions asked of (insert position applying for here)". This search should give you some great questions to practice with in addition to the ones that I provide.

How can you practice when you don't know the exact questions? Well you know the general position that you would be interested in and what field you are applying to. Using that information, along with the job description, focus on key skills and qualifications that your potential employer may desire in their "ideal" candidate. With this knowledge you can best guess which questions will be asked or at least which skill areas the questions will be catered to. (Refer to Chapter

2 if you need more help on researching the company and what is important to them.) Prepare your answers based on situations that you have experienced through your work, volunteer, and/or school experiences that would speak to those skills. You can even get out some good ol' pen and paper and create a list of great experiences that you would want to share or that you can pull from during an interview and use that list to practice explaining your experience using the STAR method.

For more information on STAR questions I recommend visiting: http://www.rasmussen.edu/student-life/blogs/main/common-interview-questions-and-answers/

5 TWENTY-FIVE INTERVIEW QUESTIONS AND WHAT THE INTERVIEWER IS LOOKING FOR IN YOUR ANSWER

I've talked with the Human Resource professionals in my life and read various guides and how-to articles. These are the 25 interview questions that I've found come up most often in my searches and discussions. In this Chapter I go over what interviewers are typically looking for in your answers by asking these questions. I do not, however, give you a script. If you are using scripted answers it will come across that way to the interviewer. These questions are also listed at the end of this book with space in true workbook style so you can jot down notes about information you would want to include should they come up during any of your interviews.

1. Can you tell me about yourself?

The reason I'm starting us off with this question is that there are very few interviews that take place that don't have some variation of this question being asked. This question can seem vague and is one that you could easily answer with too short of an answer or an answer that seemingly never ends.

That is why it is crucial to prepare for this question. You don't want to leave the interviewer wondering who you are, but you also don't want to bore them with details that they do not need. Remember, you are here to meet a need that this company has. Focus on that aspect in your answer. Prepare a pitch that is easily changed from one interview to the next that gives highlights that provide a snapshot of your education and career experiences as they apply to the specific job you are interviewing for. Emphasize two to three points that focus on why you are the most desirable candidate for this position. Be confident in your answer. You can also take lessons from marketers and advertisers in this answer. Do a little research on marketing to add an interesting twist to your answer of this question.

There are definitely some things that you should leave out of your answer, so **don't**:

- Give your life story.

- Discuss things that they aren't allowed to ask about legally anyway, such as children and childcare, medical issues, religion, marriage status, nationality, age, sexual orientation, reasons for military discharge. This potentially opens the door for discrimination.

- Take more than two minutes to answer. If you are going beyond two minutes in this question then you are probably giving more information that you need to, or you need to tighten up your reply to be more concise and to the point.

- Having trouble shortening your answer? Practice with someone, they can give you an outside view on what should go. Sometimes just having someone else help can allow you to see issues that you were oblivious to before.

Your answer to this question is going to vary for each position and company that you interview for.

2. How does your experience make you right for this job? Why should we hire you? What makes you more qualified than other candidates?

The above questions are all essentially asking the same thing, what is it that you can do for us better than the other candidates can so that we will offer you the position over them?

Even though this question can seem intimidating, it is your chance to shine. Be specific in your answers. Remember all that research from Chapter 2? This is one of the questions where it will come in handy. If you did your research you know what problems the company is looking to solve. So now tell them how you are the perfect candidate to solve those problems, what experience you have had in the past solving problems similar to theirs, and how you were successful in those endeavors. If you have thought of an exact plan of action that you feel you could execute in this position in order to benefit the company then here is the place to share that. Make sure you are excited about how you were successful and/or how you can fix their problems. A company not only wants someone who can get the job done, but someone who enjoys doing it.

Remember, an interview is not a place for modesty. This question especially needs you to put on your best marketing hat and convince the interviewer to choose the product that is you.

3. Why are you looking for a new job?/Why are you leaving your current/previous position?

You always want to put a positive perspective on this question. No matter how terrible you think your previous employer was, this is certainly not the place to go over the issues and problems that you had with him/her.

An interviewer will look at how you talk about your current/previous employer. They will not want to hire anyone who bad mouths any employer previous or current. They will worry about what you would say to others about their company if you are willing to talk badly about another.

So what should you say when answering this question?

First, you should be honest, if you were fired own up to it. But don't give any incriminating details. You can begin your answer with "Unfortunately I was let go, however, this gives me the opportunity to…" Use what you like about the company/job you are interviewing for as a basis for the remainder of your response. Go over what new opportunities you hope to experience in a new position. Show that the role you are interviewing for would be a better fit for you than your previous position.

If you left voluntarily explain why in a positive light. Again use what you like about the company/job you are interviewing for as a basis for your response.

Sub questions:

The following two questions will sometimes follow question number 3.
a.   Why were you fired?

b.   Could you explain the gap in your resume?

When answering a question about why you were fired, I highly recommend that you be honest and explain the situation and own it. Did you learn something from the experience? I hope you did and if so, now is the time to go over how you used your firing as a lesson. It looks favorably if you can take a bad situation, like getting fired, and make yourself a better potential employee because of it.

If there is an especially large gap in your resume it can make an employer skittish. They may think that you enjoyed your time out of the workforce and would soon leave the company putting them in a bind for finding and training another new employee shortly after hiring you. What they are typically looking for in an answer here is, first of all, honesty and second why you would be not only the best candidate for the job, but the job would be the best for you. If during your employment hiatus you partook in activities, volunteering, classes, etc. that gave you skills directly applicable to this type of job, make sure you include that while you were out of the work force you still did _____ and this would help you with _____ (one of the things listed in the job description should go here). Just always be sure to guide the question's answer back to how you can contribute to their organization or why you are the best candidate for the job.

4. Have you ever worked with a difficult boss/co-worker? What made the situation difficult and how did you handle it?

Just like in question number 3 anytime you are going over a negative experience in an answer for an interview question, you will want to put a positive spin on it. If you have had a difficult boss or co-worker in the past (and who hasn't had one or the other at some point) then make it into a learning experience and give the interviewer what you learned from going through that. Was it patience, better time management to be prepared for last minute tasks? The list can go on.

5. What is your greatest strength?

This question is nearly infamous as it is so regularly asked in interviews. The reason behind asking this question is fairly obvious. The recruiter wants to know what you think you are best at. And if you practice answering this beforehand with a reply that is catered to the needs of the company, well then, this is a question that you can easily ace.

To prepare for answering this question read the job description carefully. If you are more hands on like me then print it out and highlight away. Now, go over the qualities that they are looking for. Which of these qualities are you the best at? That quality from the job description should be your greatest strength or at least VERY CLOSELY related to your greatest strength in your answer to this question. To bring the answer to this question home, provide an example from previous jobs (or volunteer experience) where you demonstrated this strength.

Remember to always practice answering in a show, don't tell style.

6. What is your greatest weakness?

Like the question above, this question is asked in nearly all interviews now. If you would have asked me a few years ago what the answer to this question should be, I would have said spin a strength as a weakness, such as I work too hard, etc. However, most interviewers are now privy to this method and watch out for it.

It is only advisable to use a weakness that will not directly impact the job that you can do for this company or one that you are working on overcoming. If it is one that you are working on overcoming, share what you are doing to improve this weakness and how far you have come since you began working on it. If the company offers training that would help with your weakness, tell them that you would be very interested in attending this training in order to make yourself a better employee. If it is a weakness that would not directly reflect upon your work at this company, be sure to point that out to the interviewers.

7. Where do you see yourself in five/ten/twenty years?

The reason employers ask this question is they want to make sure they are hiring someone who is going to be interested in this job or career path for the long haul. If they are going to invest their time and money into training someone, it makes sense financially for them to hire someone who is looking to stay. This is the place to show that you have done some self-assessment and career planning.

Once upon a time in the interview tips world you would see people advising to say "I want to be where you are sitting." Well, if you are applying to an entry level position in Human Resources at this company that *might* be an okay answer.

Instead, if you have specific goals that could happen inside of that company, point them out. Maybe you hope that your work performance will have allowed you to move up the ladder at this company, actually that would be a pretty great answer. Be sure to use your knowledge from your earlier research to know what specific jobs are titled at this company. Do they have CEOs, Presidents, Directors, Managers, or something else? Company lingo can vary greatly even in the same field.

Remember in answering this questions that your main point should be on the positive difference that you would make at this company should they choose to hire you over the other candidates.

8. What is your salary history?

This question is one that is being talked about quite a lot lately. Is it one that you should even answer? Some sources say that a company shouldn't need to know your salary history to know what you are worth paying; instead you should tell them what your desired salary is. There will be some interviewers that insist upon knowing your salary history. It is entirely up to you whether you want to, or feel comfortable, answering that question.

Are you feeling bullied to answer and don't feel comfortable disclosing this information? That may be a sign that this company is not the right fit for you anyway, sometimes it is better to cut your losses than get stuck at a job/company you are miserable in.

If you feel comfortable disclosing your salary history and don't see that there would be any issue, then you should tell them what you are currently making, include any bonus amounts as well as benefits and other perks that you receive from your current job. This will help you to show them the full package of your earnings, which can be much greater than what is shown solely by the dollar amount of your salary.

If you do not want to disclose that information you can say something like, "I consider that information confidential but I'm looking for a range of…." At this point some interviewers will continue on with the interview and some will become insistent upon the salary history. What you do at that point is up to you.

Do keep in mind that there are still a number of companies out there (state and government jobs especially, in my experience) that require this question to be answered and they will not consider hiring you should you refuse to answer the question. That is something you will have to take into consideration. This is one situation where you need to assess what you feel comfortable answering/risking as this is one place where I would not tell you what you should do.

9. What salary are you looking for?

This question is different than what is your salary history as they want to know what you need to work for them. If your number and theirs is way off then they will either not consider you (your number is much higher than theirs) or they will greedily grab you up at a discount (your number is much lower than theirs.) To keep from missing an opportunity because you quoted too high of a number (unless that is what the position is truly worth) or from leaving money on the table, do your due diligence and research what the going rate is for this position with your experience in your geographical area. If you are faced with this question and you didn't have time to research (tsk, tsk) prior to the interview then you can say that you are looking for the fair market value of the position. By stating this, they may turn around and ask what you think is the fair market value, in which case you will wish you were prepared for this question. However, should this situation arise, just be honest with them and tell them that further research would need to be completed on your end.

10. Could you describe a situation where you achieved great success in your previous job?

Talk about an opportunity to toot your own horn! With this question you can really shine (or fail) during the interview process. Use the STAR method from Chapter 4 to answer this question to really be able to drive home all the points that you will want to make.

Now, you should have many achievements from your previous job(s). The situation that you use in answering this question needs to be tailored to the job that you are applying for. Or emphasize the aspects of your actions that would apply to the job you are applying for.

For example, you should emphasize leadership in a team situation if the position you are applying for is in management. This is a way to turn a success from a completely unrelated job into something relatable to the position at hand.

11. Can you give me three (or five) words that your previous boss would use to describe you?

Your answer to this question should be concise. They asked for a specific amount of words, so do not ramble on. Give them the words they need and then at the end of your answer you can ask if they need clarification on any of the descriptors that you used. I advise using words that would correlate to the position that you are applying for. But in using these words, make sure they do describe you. Otherwise if they call your previous boss for a referral and this question comes up you won't be so out of the ball park that they start to wonder if you were honest in any of your interview questions.

12. Can you give me three (or five) words you'd use to describe your work style?

Like question number 11, the answer to this should be concise. Again, you should cater the answer to this question to match the job description and at the end of your answer ask if they need any clarification on the descriptors that you used. Of course the words you use should genuinely describe your work style; you are just choosing the parts of your work style that most closely relate to the job at hand.

Another way that they may word this question is more open ended than just asking for a specific number of words. They may ask "How would you describe your work style?" If they leave the question open ended you will not need to be as concise as when they ask for a certain number of descriptors. Just remember to cater your answer to the job description, the company's values, and be your own best marketer!

13. Can you describe your dream job?

If the position you are applying to is a desk job with a lot of typing involved you will NOT want to answer this question stating that your dream job is one in which you are outside a lot and not tied to a computer.

If that is your dream job, why are you applying to the desk job anyway? That is what the hiring manager is going to think if you answer in that manner.

This question is geared for the hiring manager to know if this position is in line with your goals. They want to hire someone who will stay long term, not someone who is wishy washy about what they want to do and will soon flit off to the next best thing without ever truly giving this position their true effort.

Use what you know about the company and their culture to answer this question. Don't be dishonest, but use aspects of them and this job that you would look forward to in your description of your dream job.

14. What did you like/dislike about your previous job?

While it can be tempting to go on a rant about your previous job if you left on bad terms, please don't do that. Keep your dislikes in this answer to the things that you didn't like that you wouldn't find at the new job anyway.

When telling them about what you liked about your previous job you should focus on the aspects that you liked that you know would correlate to the position you are currently interviewing for.

15. What is your ideal working environment?

Your ideal working environment should be the one that you are applying to. This is a way that the hiring manager can make sure you are a good fit for the company and will be happy there.

This is a very important question for companies that have unusual working environments and you will typically find that those types of companies are usually the ones asking this question during the interview process to make sure you will fit in. This is where researching the culture of the company can come into play as it will give you some insight into the work environment. Which will, in turn, help you to answer this question.

16. What do you know about our company?

This question sounds a bit like a test doesn't it? Well that's because it is a test question. They want to see just how serious you are about working for them. If you don't know anything beyond what can be found on the first page of their website, then they will feel that you aren't really that interested in working for their company and are looking for just any job that you can find. You will want to vary your response depending on the position that you are applying for. If you were applying for a sales position and they were just in the news for breaking their previous sales records by X% then you should definitely include that in what you know about their company.

This question is also a good place to give some input on any issues that you see they are having and how you can help to solve those problems. You can even come in with a 30 day/90 day/6 month plan to show them how you would approach the problem and take care of it. This shows not only extreme interest, but a get up and go attitude that 99.9% of companies want their employees to have.

I do want to caution you in telling them that you see they have a problem that needs to be fixed. You don't want to word your answer in a way that makes it seem like the current employees are failing. Spin in a way that they are doing a great job, but you see they need some extra help in the ____ area and here is how you intend to do that.

17. Why do you want to work here?

This test question is for them to get a feel for how serious you are about working for them. Use the research that you conducted prior to your interview to give pointed and specific answers. Do your values align with their vision and mission statement? Then tell them that. Do they work with a charity that you hold dear to your heart? Mention that as well.

Make this question work for you. Don't ramble. But try to hit at least three reasons that cover why you want to work there.

18. How do you deal with pressure/stressful situations/tight deadlines?

Sometimes this will be asked as a scenario question. But even if they don't give a specific example and ask how you would handle it, you should have a situation prepared and use the STAR method to answer (See Chapter 4).

With this question they want to get a feel for what your work ethic is. Your answer will also depend on whether the position you are interviewing for is team based or more of a self-driven position.

19. What's a time you disagreed with a decision that was made at work?

This question is to gauge how professional you can be in a conflict type situation. In any position that you have there will, at some point or other, be a disagreement between yourself and your supervisor or one of your coworkers or subordinates. Make sure you use an example that shows you made a difference in the situation in a very positive way. Refer to the STAR method in Chapter 4 to help you create your answer to this question.

20. Where else have you applied/What other companies are you interviewing with?

Many people balk at this question being asked. You may think that it is none of their business or you could be inclined to say that they are the only place that you have applied to. In some ways it isn't their business, but the reason they ask is to gauge how serious you are in your job hunt. They are also looking to see if you are looking for a particular career or are desperate and applying to anything and everything.

The best answer to this question is to be honest, up to a point. I would only mention other places that you have applied to that are similar in nature to this position. That answer will show that you are interested in this type of career path and makes you look more reliable. For brownie points some people will begin their answer with "While your company is my first choice, I have also applied to _____." I wouldn't go into too much detail. Just make sure that you get across the point that you are serious in your job search and that your interest in the interviewer's company is very strong.

21. **What was the last book/magazine/website/article you read or documentary/television show you watched?**

This is a question that may be asked in order for the interviewer to try to get a feel on your personality, fit with the team, or to see if you are keeping up with industry news. This is one way that the interviewer can judge how committed you are to the field that you are applying to.

This question can be worded many different ways hence all the backslashes up there. Just be prepared and don't say that you've recently read a book on the industry that you haven't read. They may have follow-up questions or discussion that can out you rather quickly.

22. **How did you hear about the position?**

It would be really easy to answer this question in a short non-descript answer. But you can really shine with this question. If you heard about the position through someone who either works for the company or is a customer of the company feel free to name drop, then go on to explain what about the position caught your eye. If you saw it on a job board use the same approach. This thorough answer shows the interviewer that you are interested in the position/company and have an eye for detail.

23. Tell me about a challenge or conflict you've faced at work and how you dealt with it.

This is a good question to use the STAR Method with (see Chapter 4).

The reasoning behind this question is usually for the interviewer to judge your work ethic to see if you would be a good fit for the company culture. Like everyone, you have had challenges that you faced in previous jobs, do your best to choose one that you turned into a positive experience (or learning experience) and would most benefit you in the position you are applying to.

24. What do you like to do outside of work?

While keeping in mind that you are at a job interview and your answer will need to be professional (don't say that you live for getting trashed on Saturday night, do say that you occasionally enjoy a drink or two with friends), it is okay to be completely honest in this question. It is a way for the interviewer to see you open up and share your personality with them. This technique gives them more insight into seeing if you will fit into their culture. If you have volunteer work that you regularly participate in make sure to mention it when you answer this question. Especially mention any duties that you perform when volunteering that would correspond to job duties that you would have to perform should you obtain the position you are currently interviewing for.

25. What motivates you?

Gear this question towards the position that you are applying for. If you are applying to a job where you will be working closely with customers you may want to say that you are motivated by making sure the customer's needs are met. If you are applying to a teaching position you would want to say that seeing your students really grasp the material is your motivation. Just make sure that you don't say your motivation is money. While this may be true, it will cause you to come across as money hungry and unconcerned about doing a good job to the interviewers.

These are just the 25 most common interview questions that I have come across in learning more about the interview process. There are dozens of articles online about other common interview questions. Once you have your answers to these down pat, you may want to branch out, do an internet search, and practice other interview questions as well.

6 ILLEGAL INTERVIEW QUESTIONS

There are some questions that you may be asked that should not be asked of you. These are questions about your gender, family status, nationality, religion, sexual orientation, and/or age. How you react to these questions is up to you, but I would like to give some insight as to why and how these questions get asked (it isn't always with ill intent) and some tips on how you can gracefully respond when you are put in an uncomfortable situation.

There are situations in which the interviewer has never had training on the laws regarding the hiring process and truly do not know that what they are asking is illegal. Usually they are asking these types of questions to gauge dependability of their potential hire. If you feel that this is the situation you can choose to inform the interviewer that the question they are asking is illegal.

However, be warned as being reprimanded can leave a sour taste in their mouth regarding your interview and can cost you the position. You will need to decide ahead of time how you want to react to these questions should they come up. Being prepared will give you the ability to be more poised and not be caught off guard by a question that may hit on some sensitive areas.

So what are your options in deciding how to react to a potentially illegal interview question?

Your first option would be to answer the question as it is asked. Some people are comfortable in answering these questions and if you are one of those people then that is fine and you don't need to worry about your interaction with the interviewer. But only answer if you truly feel comfortable with providing the information.

Your second option would be to flat out refuse to answer and let the interviewer know that you feel the question is illegal and not relevant to the position. This direct answer can cut you out of the running for the job. But as I tell people in the workshop that I teach, do you really want to work at a company that is comfortable asking illegal questions during their interview process and using that answer (or refusal to answer) against you when deciding who to hire to their company. That is a decision that is completely up to you, but I know I wouldn't be.

The third option is to not really answer the question but

to answer the concern that they have behind the question.

So how do you know what their intent/concern behind the question is?

If they are asking a question regarding your intent to have children you could say that whether you have a family or not that you still intend to follow a career path. The intent of that question is to determine whether you are going to be around for the long haul and if you are going to be a dependable investment.

If the question is related to age there are many ways that you can answer. You should also be aware that there are questions that will "fish" for your age without the interviewer coming right out and asking. They may instead inquire about what year you graduated college. You could reply with "I'm not sure how that question is relevant to the job description. What information are you looking for?" Or if the question is very age specific you could simply state that your age has never been an issue in the past and that you feel confident in your ability to perform the job duties that position requires.

There are some questions regarding religion and sexual orientation that should never be asked by the interviewer and you again will have to decide on how to answer those.

All the areas of discrimination that could be asked about by an interviewer illegally are race, color, sex, religion, national origin, age, sexual orientation, and disability.

If you feel that the interviewer is asking in a malicious attempt to discriminate against potential job candidates when making their decision on who to offer the position to then you may want to report them to the Equal Employment Opportunity Commission (EEOC). For more information on the EEOC in your area visit http://www.eeoc.gov.

As long as you are prepared ahead of time for the potential of illegal interview questions you can keep your cool and answer in a professional manner. Even if that answer is to inform them of their mistake in asking those types of questions. If this costs you the job you still may save someone else the discomfort of being asked illegal interview questions.

7 CHOOSING THE RIGHT QUESTIONS TO ASK

I'm going to need you to make me a promise. I need you to promise me that under no circumstances will you ever again say "No" when you are asked if you have any questions at the end of an interview.

"Why?" you may ask.

Well, when you leave an interview without asking any questions you are leaving so much on the table and are not expressing to the interviewer that you really are the right person for the job.

In Chapter 2 we discussed that you need to know everything you possibly can about the company and the job you are applying to before your interview. Use that knowledge and create questions, at least five, before the interview ever happens. Did you read something interesting in the news that the company is developing? Ask about the future of this new product or how it will affect the department that you will be working in.

If it is allowed, please take a pen and some paper into the interview; bring your questions with you if you can. This is a great practice so that you won't forget your questions when you are put on the spot. It is also beneficial to you if during the interview any of your questions are answered, you can simply cross them off saving you from inadvertently asking them.

The only thing worse than leaving an interview without asking any questions is asking a question that has already been answered. This leaves the interviewer thinking "Was this person even listening to me?".

As for bringing a pen with you, if something comes up during the interview that you would like more clarification on you can jot down your question so that you won't forget at the end of the interview.

What are the best types of questions to ask?

Open ended questions of course! These will allow for conversation to take place between yourself and the interviewer. Conversation will make the interviewer connect with you on a more personal level and allow them to see you more favorably.

Some example questions that may be tweaked to nearly any type of interview:

- **Why did you choose to work here?**

    This question gets the interviewer to thinking nostalgically about when they first began their job here. It may even get them to sympathize with you if they remember how nervous they were during their interview.

- **What will be this position's biggest challenges in the first six months to a year?**

    This shows that you are planning on sticking around for the long haul. That you want to make sure that you are up to the task of meeting these challenges.

- **How would you describe the company team/culture?**

    This is a great question if you were unable to find much information on the company's culture or found mixed messages about their culture. Pay very close attention to the answer of this question if you were unable to get a good read on their culture during your research phase of interview preparation. Their answer will help you to decide if you would want to accept the position with the company should you be offered it.

- **How would my performance be measured?**

    This is another question that shows seriousness and dedication to the position. In asking this question you are showing that you are already thinking about how best to perform your job duties.

- **What are the development goals over the next five years?**

    This question not only shows that you are interested in the long haul, but it can give you an idea of whether the position is a temporary or more permanent one. That information can be valuable when assessing a job offer.

- **How does this role fit into the company structure?**

    Like the question above this question too can help to sniff out a temporary position. If you are looking for a job where you can settle in and stay for a while then you will want to pay close attention to the answer to these.

- **Why is the position vacant?**

    While the interviewer won't come out and say it, if you read between the lines you will be able to tell if the position is vacant due to bad management or other similar difficulties. The answer to this question will also come into play if you have a job offer to decide upon.

- **What happens next?**

   What does happen next? Do you need to call and check back in the next week? Are they the type of company that prefers the "Don't call us, we'll call you" method?

   This is good information to know so that you don't unwittingly call when they would prefer for you not to. Also, if you are supposed to go down the hall to Peggy Sue's office and do a work study or other assessment you don't want to miss out on that! They should make you aware of these types of things, but interviewers are people too and sometimes they forget to mention things. This question will help to prod their memory a little.

Now, I won't be offended if you choose not to use any of the questions that I've offered for you to use. But I do hope that you will put some time and thought into the questions that you do ask. Use these questions to show not only that you are interested in the position, but that you have already done some research. There may even be a way to work some questions in that reiterate what a good choice you would be as an employee of the company.

8 CLOSING THE INTERVIEW

As tempting as it is when the interview is over don't just sprint out of the door. You want them to feel like you aren't anxiously awaiting the time to get out of there. Here are a few things to do before you confidently excuse yourself from their presence.

The Last Minute Sell

The last minute sell is where you will try to smoothly fit in any extra information that you feel the interviewers will need to know in order to choose you as their candidate for the position. This is a great place to share a portfolio if you have one with you. A portfolio will only apply to certain careers and positions, but the majority of jobs out there can utilize a portfolio in one way or another. The last two positions that I have held I brought a portfolio with me to the interview and went through it with the interview panel.

More About the Portfolio

I personally use a 3 ring binder with page protectors for my portfolio. If you have a smaller portfolio you can use the folders with the 3 tabs. This would also be a good practice if you plan on leaving the portfolio with the interviewers.

Also, since you will be carrying your portfolio around it could easily be lost or misplaced, never put originals of anything in your portfolio. Use copies only.

What to include (these are just examples, you can include what you feel is important to the position that you are applying for):

- Resume
- Cover Letter
- Reference Page
- Letters of Recommendation
- Educational Certificates
- Certifications
- Licenses
- Degrees
- Transcripts
- Awards
- Honors
- Recognition Pieces
- Work Samples
- Project Summaries
- Employment Evaluations (feel free to leave out

any negative employment evals.)

Your portfolio can also be used when you are answering interview questions if you have an example of work that would help you to answer a question. This will add a little oomph to your answer by giving the interviewer something concrete to judge your talents by.

Good Handshake

You will want to leave with a good strong hand shake. But make sure that you do not have too firm of a grasp nor too soft of one.

Keep in mind that if you tried to shake the interviewer's hand at the beginning of the interview and they declined, then you should not try to shake their hand again.

Display Confidence

When you leave the interview you need to leave it with your body language demonstrating that you feel confident in how well you did during the interview process. Head up, shoulders back, no slumping, and do not drag your feet or shuffle out of the door.

Even if you feel like you did everything wrong during the interview you still need to walk out like you did well. For all you know the interviewers didn't pick up on your mistakes and thought you did a good job. If you leave like you are defeated, you may leave them wondering what it was that they missed.

9 THE FOLLOW UP

Following are some recommendations for following up with the company after your interview.

Thank You Card

Why send a thank you card?

A thank you card will bring your name back up in the mind of the interviewer. If they are debating between you and one other person, then the thank you card can give a little extra oomph in coming out on top if your competition does not send one.

A thank you card can also be used to address any information that you forgot to share during the interview and that you feel would help the interviewer decide to choose you.

And in a worst case scenario a thank you card can also

be used to smooth over a question that you blew or an awkward moment during the interview (maybe your internet went out during the middle of a Skype interview).

For the thank you card, I recommend already having one in your car with the envelope addressed and stamped. You can then write the thank you while everyone's names and highlights from the interview are fresh in your mind. Stop by the post office and mail it on your way home from the interview. Just don't forget the stamp! It would not look good for them to have to pay to receive your thank you card, although, I bet they wouldn't forget your name if that happened…

Is it ever okay to send an email thank you? In this day and age there are certainly times that you can send your thank you through email. If your correspondence with the company has all been electronic up to this point then it would be appropriate to send an emailed thank you.

However, an actual card could potentially stand out if your competitors for the position are all also sending an emailed thank you.

Phone Call (later)

I personally wait at least a week before giving a phone call to check in. People are busy and your interviewer is not excluded from a busy work load. This phone call will remind the interviewer of you and will show that you are still interested in the position.

Do keep in mind that some companies will request that you not contact them to inquire about the job. Respect that request or you will show them that you do not know how to listen and that can be a potentially disqualifying trait in a job candidate.

Do what you said you could do!

If you get the job then make sure that you do what you said you could do. If you told them that you are a pro at Excel you don't want to be asking beginner questions when you receive your first assignment. Make sure you are up to the task before accepting the position, and then when you are in your new office, blow them away with your amazing skills. Remind them why they chose you. Don't make your new boss regret his/her decision or you may find yourself quickly starting over at square one in the job hunting process.

10 A BRIEF SOCIAL MEDIA DISCUSSION

As promised earlier I will go over a little bit on social media and how it can affect your job hunt. Technically speaking if you've already landed an interview, your potential employer most likely has already searched out your social media profiles and viewed what wasn't set to private. However, I still feel that this is an important topic to hit on. Especially with the ever increasing popularity of social media.

There are literally hundreds, possibly even thousands, of social media outlets online. I'm just going to briefly go over some tips that are geared towards the most popular ones and the ones that I have personally had experience in using. These tips should easily be transferred to other social sites though. After following the tips I do recommend doing an internet search on your name and usernames to make sure you didn't miss any old forgotten social media outlets you may have used in years past. (Myspace anyone?)

Why is it so important that you look at what you are portraying yourself as on social media anyway?

In this day and age the majority of employers are going to check out your social media sites. Some of these same employers are also viewing it as a warning sign if you don't have anything about yourself on social media or if all of your profiles are in super lock down private mode.

Spring Cleaning

Ah, the good ol' cleaning up of your online presence. You are going to want to be sure that you clean up anything on your online profiles that insinuate alcohol/drug abuse, bad mouthing former employers or bad mouthing in general, provocative photos, political posts that are divisive, and anything that is hateful, unprofessional, or just generally damaging to the professional image that you want to portray.

When cleaning up and improving your profiles realize that the main reason behind searching social media profiles is that companies can do a quick and dirty background check on you through your social media accounts. They can use them to see if what you are portraying to the public matches up to what you are saying on your resume/application.

Some profiles you may not want to clean up because they are not to be used for professional matters. These sites (Facebook and Instagram for example) can and should be set to private.

Job Hunting

Social media is a great place to actually perform your job hunt. In Chapter 2 we discussed using social media to learn more about the company you are interviewing with, but you can also use social media to follow companies that you would be interested in working for.

Many companies now post their open jobs on sites like LinkedIn, Twitter, and sometimes even Facebook. You can also use these sites to network with people who work at the company you are interested in. By keeping in touch with them you may hear about job openings before they are posted.

Other companies will actually use social media to find people that they think would be good for a job opening that they have prior to posting it. So make sure your profiles have all the correct key words and that your career history is updated and accurate in your profile. You will also want to post projects that you have worked on, articles you have written, acknowledgements, and awards that you have received.

Keep in mind that if you are employed elsewhere and don't want anyone to know that you are looking for employment with another company then you will want to not publically post anything about your job search. Keep all that information in private messages and emails and off of public forum.

Use as an Online Resume

Keep your social media profiles updated with your past and current employment. You should definitely update (and make public on all sites) big job accomplishments that you would want a potential employer to be aware of.

Many employers also peruse your social media sites to get a feel for what your personality and demeanor are like. Make sure to showcase that in some of your posts. Show them what makes you unique. Interact in groups and share things that you find interesting. Just make sure to keep it professional.

If you have any doubts about what you've posted you should probably take it down or make it private. You can also turn to a trusted friend and get their opinion, especially if they work in the Human Resource field.

11 INTERVIEW TYPES

I saved this chapter for near the end of the book because regardless of the interview type the preparation and practice for the interview is basically going to be the same.

Following are the different types of interviews and what they may look like for you.

Apprentice Interview: this interview is one in which you may expect to complete an actual job task or work study. The interviewers want to see how your work compares to what you say you can do. This is one place where you can really shine if you go in prepared to impress with your mad skills.

Behavior Based Interview: This is what it sounds like, it is an interview in which the interviewer will ask you questions that determine your behavior in situations on the theory that past performance will predict future performance. In a behavior based interview you should rely heavily on the STAR method (Chapter 4) of answering interview questions. Take no more than 3-5 minutes to answer each question. It is very easy to become long winded (and subsequently boring) when answering these types of questions.

Case Based Interview: In this type of interview you will be given a problem, puzzle, or a business case and be asked to solve it. This gives the interviewer an example of your technical knowledge, creativity, strategic thinking, leadership skills, and an example of your ability to perform under pressure. I recommend that in solving the problem when you give your answer you not only give your solution, but also include the method by which you arrived to that solution and why that solution would be the best for this particular situation. This will give the interviewer a bigger view into your thought process and will (hopefully) impress them more than just spitting out a solution.

Dinner/Lunch Interview: This interview is usually a second or third interview and is a really good sign that the company is interested in you and is using this to better determine your fit within the company.

However, don't let that information go to your head; you will still need to prepare for this interview just like any other. But there are a few extra things to keep in mind. Since the company will be picking up the tab for the bill, try to stay in the mid-price range for your meal selection. Don't choose soup (too much slurping potential), spaghetti, ribs, or any other especially messy food. Be sure to take small bites as you want to be able to quickly chew and swallow your food without difficulty when a question is asked of you. And seriously, if you are a huge bite taker, your risk of choking and needing the Heimlich maneuver performed on you in front of your potential future employer greatly increases.

Personally, I think after being saved from near death I would then turn around and die from embarrassment in that situation. But, hey, that's just me.

Oh and one more thing, just in case I have to say it, don't order alcohol at a meal interview. Seriously, don't. Save that for celebrations with your friends and family after you accept the job offer.

Group Interview: Now here is a fun experience, especially for those of us who are more shy, meek, or introverted in nature; a group interview is just that, a group of potential employees being interviewed at the same time by the potential employer. You will typically see this in larger companies that are trying to fill more than one open position of the same role (think call center, medical interns, sales roles, consultants, etc.).

In a group interview the interviewer is also trying to see how the interviewees interact with the other candidates. Who seems to be falling into the leadership role? Who is the one thinking outside of the box? Which one(s) just do things when they are told to do? And so on.

None of the above scenarios are necessarily best, it just depends on which personality the company thinks will fit the role. But you will want to try to stand out in some way so that the interviewers notice you above the other candidates. Once you've made it through the group interview process you may have an individual based interview.

Job Fair Interview: This interview type is just what it sounds like. You will go to a job fair or similar event where employers are set up giving out information on the positions that they currently have open.

When attending these events you ideally have copies of your resume with you. Once the employer reviews your resume he or she may have a few questions for you, interview style, as a prescreening to determine whether or not they will be calling you for an official interview in the future. So you will want to brush up on your interview question answering prior to attending any of these events during your job search.

The only part that will be different for this interview is unless you know ahead of time which companies will be there you may not be able to perform any research regarding their culture, issues, etc. Just read over the information they hand you quickly and try to implement that in your answers so that you can cater to their needs as much as possible when answering. But do not despair, this isn't an official interview, so just do your best and make sure that you take notes after the fact so that you can better prepare if you get called in for an official interview at the company.

The longest one of these interviews will last is roughly 15 minutes, most will be much shorter, so be sure to be ready to market yourself to the employer.

Panel Interview (also referred to by many as the firing squad): This is one interview setting that the majority of people find to be a bit intimidating. In this interview situation you are typically seated on one side of a table, or at the head of a table depending on the size of the panel, while you are faced with three or more interviewers.

Each person on the panel will usually have their own interview questions for you, but you will want to try to make eye contact with all, or at least several, of the people on the panel during your answers. These interviewers may represent several different departments at the company where you are interviewing. Usually, they will consist of the departments that your position will affect or interact with the most.

Just to give you a heads up, many state and government based jobs will have a panel style interview. Or this has been my experience when applying and interviewing at these types of facilities.

Phone Interview: The phone interview tends to be very informal and like the Job Fair Interview it is used to verify that you are a candidate that they would want to invite in for an official interview.

I will note that in some cases, where you are going to be working online or are currently too far to drive to the interview, a phone interview can be the official interview.

But, even if the phone interview is being used as a

screening tool you will still want to treat it very seriously and practice for it just as you would for the main event. I recommend calling someone to actually practice the interview on the phone from the location that you will be in during the interview. This can help pick up on weird background noises, echoes, phone service, etc. Also, practicing on the phone will allow you to practice using your voice to get the point across. In a phone interview they will not be able to see your body language or facial expressions. So you will need to rely solely on your voice to get all of your points across.

Take a lot of notes during the phone interview. Anything that you think you may want to practice more or research further to help you out during the official interview will be beneficial to write down, so long as you plan to act on it.

Situational Interview: This is where the interviewer asks you questions about situations that you have found yourself in, or that you may find yourself in and what you did or what you would do.

These questions are where you are going to want to pull out the STAR method (Chapter 4) of answering interview questions.

These questions are used to determine what type of experience you have and whether or not you will be able to fulfill the job requirements.

Occasionally the Behavior Based Interview and the Situational Interview will overlap.

Stress Interview: I've been fortunate enough to have never experienced the stress interview. It is typically seen in interviews for those being hired at the top of the food chain, company presidents, CEOs, etc. So maybe, I've not actually been fortunate to have not experienced this interview as I'm definitely not the top dog at any company currently.

In this interview type you are put on the spot in an effort to see what your reaction is when you are under pressure. Do you react creatively, positively and search for a solution, do you get angry and give attitude, or do you stammer and look to others for the solution?

There's really no way to determine in what way the interviewers will try to throw you under the bus, if you suspect that this is the type of interview you may face, I encourage you to search stress interviews in relation to the industry you are interviewing in and use that knowledge to help you when following my steps to prepare for the interview.

Structured Interview: Many people are familiar with this type of interview. It is a face to face interview where you are asked multiple questions in relation to the position that you will be filling as well as follow up questions in relation to your answers. A lot of the questions that you will find in this type of interview can be answered with STAR method found in Chapter 4. The structural interview is quite similar to the traditional interview except that the questions tend to be more concise, versus the broad nature of the traditional interview questions.

Traditional Interview: I'm sure almost everyone reading this book has been through at least one traditional interview, or seen one on a show or in a movie. This is the interview where they ask the typical, broad interview questions that can be asked about almost any position in an attempt to determine if the interviewee has the skills and abilities to perform the job. The interviewer will also be gauging your personality and work ethic during this interview as well.

This interview is usually done one on one, but I still would consider just two to be a traditional interview.

Many interviews you experience are not going to be just one interview type. They could be a mixture of traditional and situational and so on. Just be sure that you practice and prepare yourself mentally for whatever situation you may find yourself in once you walk through the company's doors.

12 FAST TIPS FOR A SECOND INTERVIEW

So what is a second interview and what does it mean for you?

A second interview is a is a chance not only for the interviewer to make sure that you are going to be a great fit for the company, but for you to have another chance to prove that you are a great fit for the company. For you the second interview means that you did well in your first interview (CONGRATULATIONS). But don't let that go to your head and blow this chance by becoming too confident and coming across as a know-it-all or a braggart.

When you get that phone call to set up the second interview (or email depending on the company's preferred communication method) you need to ask how long the interview process will take, sometimes the second interview can take several hours to an entire day if the management wants to give you a tour of the grounds and introduce you to the people you will be working with should you score the job. There may even be an agenda for the day. This will help you know how you should plan your day, lunch, and what shoes to wear. I wouldn't advise wearing your most uncomfortable stilettoes if it looks like you are going to be doing a lot of walking.

Preparing for the second interview:

When you begin to prepare for your second interview you will want to start with the notes that you took during the first interview.

Where did you feel your answers could have been stronger? Focus on practicing answering questions that could hit on those same topics. Also practice giving slightly different answers to interview questions as some of the questions may be the same as the first interview, but you don't want to sound like a broken record.

Do more research on the company. See if anything new has come up about them in the news since the last interview. Delve a little deeper into information that you didn't have time to study during your initial research. Use this research to create new questions.

Once you have prepared using your notes and have done more research, continue preparing the same way you did in the first interview, just do so more intensively.

The second interview is likely going to have more opportunity for you to ask questions of the interviewer and have general conversation with your potential employer and future coworkers. Use this time wisely.

Here's what may be different:

You may be interviewed by different people than those who were in your first interview. Don't assume that all the information that you gave during the first interview was passed along to these folks. Make sure to include all of your relevant skills when answering the questions, not just the ones you wished you had mentioned during the first interview. You can phrase it along the lines of:

"In the last interview I mentioned _____, but I would also like to point out/add _____."

The second blank is where you will add more detail or experiences to your last interview in order to give the interviewer a better overall view of your capabilities. When going over what you stated in the last interview, just give a very short summary to avoid too much repetition of the same in case they do have a copy of what you stated previously.

There may be a workplace tour during the second interview. If the interviewer is getting serious about possibly hiring you, they will sometimes take you around to see the facility and to meet the people that you will be working with. Treat all of this as part of the interview. When people you meet ask you questions answer them in the same professional manner as you would have if you were still in the interview room.

There could be more behavioral questions, tests or work studies, off the wall questions, etc. The second interview is typically going to be harder as the employer attempts to narrow down the cream of the crop to the pick of the litter. (I apologize for the corny wording, but I find those phrases sum it up quite nicely.)

There may also be questions about anything you were unable to answer fully the first time. This is where that extra practice to hone your weak spots will come in handy.

You may be offered the job on the spot. I recommend not answering right away, get all the details that you need, ask when they need a decision by and take some time and think about it. Remember, you will want time to evaluate them and whether you feel that you would be happy there. This is a two way street. They not only need to be happy having you as an employee, but you also need to be happy to call them your employer.

Things to keep in mind:

Make sure you practice just as much, or more so, than you did for the first interview.

Be prepared for the questions to be much more in depth and difficult than they were in the first interview.

Make sure that you clear up any issues or loose ends that you felt were left after the first interview.

Just because you have the second interview doesn't mean that you are guaranteed the job, avoid being overly cocky.

Don't repeat your answers from the first interview verbatim, use this time to give additional information that will help you to secure the position.

Be prepared to discuss salary and benefits if the discussion comes up. These items are more likely to be brought up during the second interview than they were in the first.

If during the interview you feel that maybe this place is not for you, don't feel pressured to accept an offer. Take your time to think about it and get back to the employer. Even if the opposite is true and you are ready to jump on board you still may want to take a little time to think about the offer and possibly counteroffer.

Good luck during your second interview!

13 A QUICK OVERVIEW

Just to go back over a few dos and don'ts during the actual interview. Use this section as a quick refresher when you need it.

Dos:

- Practice
- Sit up straight
- Listen attentively
- Maintain good eye contact during the interview
- Sit still in your seat; avoid fidgeting and slouching
- Respond to questions and back up your statements about yourself with specific examples whenever possible (STAR Method, see Chapter 4.)
- Ask for clarification if you don't understand a question

- Be thorough in your responses, while being concise in your wording
- Be honest and be yourself, your best professional self
- Send a thank you card

Don'ts:

- Go in unprepared
- Answer questions too quickly
- Take too long to answer questions
- Make excuses
- Make negative comments
- Falsify applications or answers to questions
- Treat the interview casually
- Act like location/salary/benefits are the only importance of the job
- Act desperate
- Call if they request no contact during their decision making process

During the interview process keep in mind that your application/resume showed that you have the skills they are looking for. If not, then you wouldn't be in the "hot seat". It is your job to sell yourself, your work ethic, and your fit into their culture. Do your best to not to be nervous. Practicing as much as possible beforehand can help to alleviate some of those nerves.

I WISH YOU THE BEST OF LUCK!

25 QUESTIONS WORKSHEET

1. Can you tell me about yourself?

_____

_____

_____

_____

_____

_____

2. How does your experience make you right for this job? Why should we hire you? What makes you more qualified than other candidates?

_____

_____

_____

_____

_____

_____

3. Why are you looking for a new job?/Why are you leaving your current/previous position?

_____

_____

_____

_____

_____

4. Have you ever worked with a difficult boss/co-worker? What made the situation difficult and how did you handle it?

_____

_____

_____

_____

_____

5. What is your greatest strength?

___

___

___

___

___

___

___

6. What is your greatest weakness?

___

___

___

___

___

___

___

7. Where do you see yourself in 5/10/20 years?

_____

_____

_____

_____

_____

_____

8. What is your salary history?

_____

_____

_____

_____

_____

_____

_____

9. What salary are you looking for?

_____

_____

_____

_____

_____

_____

_____

10. Could you describe a situation where you achieved great success in your previous job?

_____

_____

_____

_____

_____

_____

_____

11. Can you give me three (or five) words that your previous boss would use to describe you?

_____

_____

_____

_____

_____

_____

12. Can you give me three (or five) words you'd use to describe your work style?

_____

_____

_____

_____

_____

_____

13. Can you describe your dream job?

_____

_____

_____

_____

_____

_____

_____

_____

14. What did you like/dislike about your previous job?

_____

_____

_____

_____

_____

_____

_____

_____

15. What is your ideal working environment?

_____

_____

_____

_____

_____

_____

_____

16. What do you know about our company?

_____

_____

_____

_____

_____

_____

_____

17. Why do you want to work here?

_____

_____

_____

_____

_____

_____

_____

_____

18. How do you deal with pressure/stressful situations/tight deadlines?

_____

_____

_____

_____

_____

_____

19. What's a time you disagreed with a decision that was made at work?

_____

_____

_____

_____

_____

_____

20. Where else have you applied/What other companies are you interviewing with?

_____

_____

_____

_____

_____

_____

21. What was the last book/magazine/website/article you read or documentary/television show you watched?

_____

_____

_____

_____

_____

_____

22. How did you hear about this position?

_____

_____

_____

_____

_____

_____

_____

23. Tell me about a challenge or conflict you've faced at work and how you dealt with it.

_____

_____

_____

_____

_____

_____

_____

24. What do you like to do outside of work?

_____

_____

_____

_____

_____

_____

25. What motivates you?

Notes:

Helpful Resources

Some of my favorite websites to visit when I'm looking for job hunting, resume, interview, and career advice are:

Themuse.com

Forbes.com

Glassdoor.com

LinkedIn.com

Salary.com

There are many more sites out there that will be beneficial to you. I recommend starting with the above websites and go from there.

Crystal Vaughan

ABOUT THE AUTHOR

In addition to having a husband and daughter that she adores, she has two cats who drive her a little crazy.

Crystal Vaughan also has a varied career background. One of her career stops had involved her in teaching Interview Skills and Resume Writing workshops at one of her previous jobs with the state of Virginia. She also writes fiction and poetry under a pseudonym.

www.ingramcontent.com/pod-product-compliance
Lightning Source LLC
Chambersburg PA
CBHW070323190526
45169CB00005B/1724